Cover
Mayfair, Fairylands

Bermuda B.C.
(before the car)

D1377917

Bermuda Impressions

William Berchen

Text by
Ursula Berchen

BAXTER'S LIMITED • BERMUDA

HASTINGS HOUSE, PUBLISHERS • NEW YORK

South Shore, Tucker's Town

Acknowledgements:

To Isabel Leonard, William Grimes and Carole
and Joseph Keating for editorial assistance and
proofreading; with special gratitude to the Keatings
for their patient labors.

First published in the U.S.A. 1976 by Hastings
House Publishers, Inc.

Baxter's Limited, P.O. Box 1009,
Hamilton, 5, Bermuda

Library of Congress Cataloging in Publication Data
  Berchen, William
  Bermuda Impressions.
  1. Bermuda Islands. I. Berchen, Ursula, joint
  author. II. Title.
F1631.B475 972.99 76-18709
ISBN 0-8038-0774-0

Published simultaneously in Canada
by Saunders of Toronto, Ltd.,
Don Mills, Ontario

Printed and bound in Italy by
Mondadori, Editore, Verona

Book design William Berchen

Typography design Arthur Howe

Typeface *Goudy*,
County Photo Compositing

Coral wall, Hamilton

Foreword

Do you remember your first sight of these sundrenched, windswept isles, which lie so open to the light of heaven that everything is etched in an unbelievable clarity, almost unbearable in its intensity? Do you remember the symphony that is a Bermuda chimney, with its glistening clearcut angles against a depth of sky? The frescoed beauty of bare branches patterning themselves in welcome contrast to the spires of sombre cedars? The lanes and alleys of little towns, roads bowered in oleanders, or shut in by high walls festooned with morning glory and nightblooming cereus? Or, more typical still, the breath-taking shock the South Shore always holds, its brilliant depths ringed with a dark horizon?

Perhaps one needs the mind of a poet and a dreamer to see these things at all, or, more important still, to see them urgently afresh with each new glimpse. Between the covers of this book, William Berchen has translated them into permanent reminders for you.

For those who retain the magic of fresh vision, this book will be a solace. Mr. Berchen's pictures eschew the obvious. There are no hackneyed views of the usual Bermuda scenes. The pictures are not a collected equivalent of the kind of card on which the tourist marks the place he occupied! Instead, each is an original expression of the recognition of the fact of beauty, set, as it happens, against a Bermuda backdrop. As such, they will be studied, again and again, in growing admiration and affection. The realization that the locale *is* merely incidental—completely secondary to the fact that each picture represents sheer beauty irrespective of its setting—means that this book will be an inspiration and a joy, a voice that sings of far places, even to those who have never left their own busy city streets. Perhaps especially to them. For all of us need, at times, the nostalgic reminder of the remote, the far, the unattainable, as a kind of dream refuge from reality. Wasn't it Carlyle who said that "a vein of poetry exists in the hearts of all men"? Here then are our dreams, here our vision of poetry —the poetry of light and shade, rhythm and design with its universal appeal.

No, this is hardly even a good Gift Book. Those who buy it to send to less fortunate friends who have never visited the Islands, will end by retaining it themselves as consolation for having to return to more prosaic surroundings; with, at the best, the laconic promise: "Wait till I show you my Bermuda book."

Terry Tucker
Bermuda Historical Society

Paradise found

The word "Bermuda," like the name of a distant beloved, creates a mental picture of beauty, fulfilment and peace. But this has been so only since early in the seventeenth century, when the island gave up her secret and was revealed to be a temptress rather than a shrew. Islands, removed as they are from a prosaic mainland, are easily credited with having mysterious, ethereal inhabitants; and being in an exposed situation, they are more subject to forces and "influences." The Bermudas were notorious for being surrounded by vicious rocks, infested with devils, and haunted by fairies. As Europeans ranged the globe, full of zeal to conquer, or driven by a combination of curiosity, greed, and courage, and on their way to make maps or history, the hundreds of ships that found themselves in the general vicinity of the island all did their damnedest to avoid the place.

The official discoverer was a Spaniard, Juan de Bermudez, in the early fifteen hundreds, and after this there were sporadic plans to colonize the island; but most people who managed to clamber ashore without being bashed on the rocks were mainly concerned with making a vessel in which to get off again, and apparently none of the settlements lasted very long.

Although many, many ships have stumbled over Bermuda and come to grief, others who were trying to reach the island found it maddeningly evasive. In the nineteenth century two British ships, seventeen years apart, sought the place, but after hunting fruitlessly— for three weeks in one case and five in the other—they were baffled and fed up. Obviously somebody at the Admiralty was having them on. Even now a surprising number of people are anything from vague to abysmal over the island's position, historical and geographical, and Bermudians would like it understood that they do not live in Europe, Africa, Texas, or the West Indies. They live about 650 miles east of Savannah—or is it Charleston?

Among those who were not entranced with the island when they did get there was Saint Brendan in the sixth century. Voyaging with his monks to find the land promised to the saints, he is said to have stopped in Bermuda; however, finding it inhabited by fiends, he crossed it off his list and continued the search elsewhere. Perhaps he now knows that the island is full of very friendly people who have named a hospital and a pilot boat after him.

The first Englishman to fetch up on Bermuda was Henry May, and even his arrival at the end of 1593 was purely accidental, due to strong waters being taken aboard his ship, and even more potent ones surrounding it. Almost untouched by man, the island was a sanctuary with a superabundance of nearly every needed food. For several months, while they built a new vessel, May and his two dozen French shipmates subsisted on plentiful fish, hefty turtles, palmetto berries, and birds. They didn't think the skinny wild swine worth bothering with. (These creatures had either survived a previous shipwreck, or had been put ashore at some time by the Spanish "for increase," and had evidently obliged). At that time the cedars were magnificent, yielding twelve-foot boards, thirty-six inches wide. When their new eighty-ton cedar ship was ready, the Frenchmen caulked it with turtle oil and lime, and with Henry May aboard they all left Bermuda for Cape Breton on May 11, 1594. After he eventually got home to England, this "worthy mariner" published the first story of Bermuda, whose every aspect was ultimately to be recorded for posterity by one writer or another.

In the summer of 1609 Bermuda acquired another group of fortuitous settlers, this time all of them English. They thought they were heading somewhere else, but seventeenth century navigation was still like that; and with storms, shoals, scurvy, syphilis, malaria, and dysentery to polish off up to a quarter of a ship's crew, only a small proportion of vessels ever reached port at all. On June 2 the three-hundred-ton *Sea Venture* had left Plymouth, in Devon, under the command of Admiral Sir George Somers, accompanied by eight smaller ships. Between them they carried over five hundred people and ample supplies to reinforce the ailing colony in Virginia. With Sir George in the *Sea Venture* was Sir Thomas Gates, who was to be Lieutenant Governor of Virginia; he and the Admiral had a financial interest in the scheme. Also aboard were Captain Christopher Newport, as third in command, and William Strachey, who was slated to be Secretary of the new colony. The Company of South Virginia had just obtained a new charter from the Crown since earlier attempts at colonizing Virginia had been a fiasco. A great deal of money had been contributed to this newest project by more than seven hundred people—noblemen, gentlemen-of-fortune, merchants, and companies of mechanics—and all of them were very excited and had high hopes of their investment.

The little fleet had instructions from the investors not to take the old route by way of the Canaries and the West Indies, but to sail directly to southern Virginia; at that time the whole east coast of North America was known as Virginia. But the *Sea Venture* blundered far south into excessive heat—so much so that "many of the people were taken with calentures. In two ships thirty-two persons died; others suffered severely, and one vessel only was free from sickness." "Calentures" was delirium, or a heat-induced fever, in which sailors supposedly saw the sea as a green field, and would jump into it.

After about eight weeks at sea "began a violent tempest—accompanied by a horrid darkness…" The flagship became separated from the fleet (not for the first time in Somers' career) and "received a mighty leak, and the ship, having spewed out her oakum from every joint almost, suddenly grew five feet deep with water above her ballast…" It was immediately evident that they must get rid of the water, or sink; so "there were seen Master, Master's Mate, Boatswain, Quartermaster, Coopers, Carpenters, and who not, with candles in their hands, creeping along the ribs, viewing the sides, searching every corner and listening in every place, if they might hear the water running in… At length one in the gunner room was mended with I know not how many pieces of beef. But to no purpose; the leak which drank in the greatest quantity of water could not be found, nor ever was. The waters still increasing, at length the pumps were choked with bringing up quantities of whole biscuit—indeed all we had, ten thousand weight." This led to a search in the bread room with the carpenter ripping up the whole room, but still the leak could not be traced.

There were about 150 people in the ship, and Strachey was impressed that there was not a male passenger, gentleman or other, but did his fair share of the labor with the pumps and bailing, even those who had never done an hour's work in their lives.

The little ship was particularly unmanageable as trunks, chests, ordnance, and barrels of beer, wine, oil, cider and vinegar had all been jettisoned. The force of one particularly huge sea "was so violent that it carried the helmsman from the helm and wrested the whipstaff out of his hand. When he attempted to seize it again, it so flew from side to side, and so tossed him from starboard to larboard that it was God's mercy it had not split him." Earlier in the storm, before the sails were taken down, even "eight men were not enough to hold the whipstaff in the steerage, and the tiller below in the gunner room." (The whipstaff was a lever to increase the power on the tiller arm. It was the helm in Elizabethan ships, before the wheel was invented). Huge waves loomed up, then slammed down on the helpless ship. After some time she was 'pooped': a gigantic wave washed her from stem to stern; the crew's feet were swept from under them. "The waters like whole rivers did flood the air" and the passengers wailed and prayed, certain they would perish either from the sea or the sky, but the sounds of their outcries were snatched away into the screaming wind. After endless hours of battering, the *Sea Venture* was "rent in pieces and absolutely lost." ("All lost! to prayers, to prayers;...Mercy on us! We split, we split!..."—*The Tempest*). During one night the superstitious seamen were disquieted even more to see the fire of their patron Saint Elmo, flickering among the sails (or was it Ariel?). But the Admiral kept faithful watch throughout the three days and four nights of "perpetual horror," while Sir Thomas Gates directed the pumps and bailing. Then "the crew, worn out with fatigue and despairing of life, broached the strong liquors, and took leave of each other with an inebriating draught, till many

of them fell asleep. In this dreadful extremity, Sir George discovered land; the news of which awoke and revived them, and every man exerted himself to do his duty."

Now it was a choice between drowning and being wrecked on the dreaded rocks, but the sailors hoisted the remains of the sails and did their best to urge the defeated ship toward the shore, where she became wedged between two rocks, as upright "as if she had been in the stocks." It was July 28, 1609 and they were off the eastern shore of Bermuda. The storm suddenly subsided; everyone was completely exhausted, but alive and in one piece—they had "no drowning mark" upon them, so all the men, women, and children were put ashore as quickly as could be managed, and so were the pigs "preserved" from the wreck. There wasn't a soul to welcome the people, but the pigs' behavior soon revealed their awareness of their own species of inhabitants on the island.

Slow, delighted smiles must have spread on many faces, as everyone stood on dry land and looked about, after so long a time of privation, cramped quarters, inconvenience, and fear. The view still consisted of rather too much sea, but there was a pattern of intermittent islands covered with bushes and trees; the sun was shining; birds were singing; the bays looked as if they contained plenty of fish, and the breeze carried whiffs of perfume, which was a special treat after all those weeks of smelling the ocean—and one's fellow passengers. Such a feeling of relief ran through the survivors that they found new reserves of energy. Orders were given, and the small boats made trip after trip between the wreck and the shore, until most of the cargo and some of the gear were landed to make the nucleus of a temporary home. Nor would these

God-fearing people neglect to give thanks to the Almighty for sparing them, and to claim for King James these strange and beautiful islands where the fates had carried them.

In *The Tempest*, Shakespeare's "vn-inhabited island" was uncharted as well, and he could locate it anywhere he pleased; but although he described weather that fitted the Mediterranean, he had the Bermudas in mind. He may have heard sailors' gossip in taverns; he was closely connected with the Earls of Southampton and Pembroke, leaders of the Virginia Company; Silvanus Jourdain's account of the island was published in 1610; or quite possibly Shakespeare had read the "true reportory of the wracke" by William Strachey, who had lodgings near the theater. Somehow the playwright knew that Bermuda, though undeniably rocky, was far from being inhabited by devils and haunted by fairies, but was really a paradise, with fruits, fish, tortoises, tame birds (the fairies), and hogs (the devils). Perhaps Shakespeare had heard as well that fresh water was "very scant," but that "musketas and flies" were "too busie"; that there were "Cacarootches" and ants; and that there was poison ivy on the island at that time; but anyway, he romantically mixed long-standing ideas about Eden with his personal concept of the New World, and gave Caliban the reassuring lines "Be not afeard; the isle is full of noises,/Sounds and sweet airs that give delight and hurt not."

The shipload from the *Sea Venture* that was about to sample these pleasures was a very miscellaneous collection. Among them were gentlefolk, a clergyman, and many from "the lower orders" (whose labors have always been the pivot upon which society turns), but if they were all to survive, a plantation must be set up right away. There were lashings of fish and fruit, though nothing like the familiar English vegetables, and no inhabitants to frighten the stranded travellers—nor to instruct them. Luckily, the leaders had been chosen for their ability.

Although Newport was "a vain, empty, conceited man" and may have been a pompous bore, naval officers were expected to make decisions. Somers was "of approved fidelity and indefatigable industry…" and both men were thoroughly seasoned from years in Queen Elizabeth's navy. Gates had voyaged with Drake to America, and all three of them had expected to have innumerable problems to solve in Virginia. Strachey had his own abilities, and was the first in a family that has had an interest in public concerns and an aptitude for administration. His literary gifts, which filtered down through the generations to Lytton Strachey, enabled him to write a vivid description of the wreck and of the locale; he wanted "to deliver the world of a foul and general error" about Bermuda, and how could he know what he was starting? The letter found its way to England the following year, with a vellum map of the island's nineteen square miles, expertly made by Somers, and announced to the investors (who "were intent on present gains") that the *Sea Venture* had not gone to the bottom after all.

The castaways were perfectly content to settle Bermuda rather than Virginia, in spite of the exasperating smaller wildlife. Everything was plentiful to sustain a colony, except fresh water, whose "gushings and soft bubblings" were far from adequate. But it didn't take long to find a substitute for drinking water, as the palmetto palm has a stem whose juice converted very satisfactorily into intoxicating bibbie. As Edmund Waller later wrote: "The sweet palmitoes a new Bacchus yield." Sir Thomas shot the local birds, and understood about salting fish, which the Admiral caught in prodigious amounts: "in half an hour he took so many… as did suffice the whole company one day." Some of those Bermuda fish were surprisingly strong, too. Somers nearly got pulled into the sea by one of them and a few years later one "William Millington was drawn into the sea by a fish and never after seen." Somers also hunted with the ship's dog, and showed his countrymen how to dispatch the swine which these settlers evidently did not look down upon, as in the summer the pigs must have been better upholstered than when Henry May saw them. There were turtle eggs, and "Prickell peares," and berries. Plants were found that caused vomiting, diarrhea, or "continence," meaning sexual restraint (or more likely, just lack of the urge). Other plants would either burn the stomach or soothe it. All of these were presumably found by the trial and error method. There was no "nimble marmozet" that Caliban spoke of, but there was "a kind of webfooted fowl…made strange hollow and harsh howling"; or in a more recent idiom they made "yelps like a hurt puppy"—"Cahow!" Hence their modern name. Strachey called them sea owls, but they were the famous fairies, masquerading as plump and trusting petrels, with a thirty-five-inch wing span and black caps, who laid hen-sized eggs in shallow burrows, and offered themselves for dinner. "Our men found a pretty way to take them, which was by standing on the rocks by the seaside, and hollowing, laughing, and making the strangest outcry that possibly they could. With the noise whereof the birds would come flocking to that place and settle upon the very arms of him that cried, and still creep nearer and nearer, answering the noise themselves;

by which our men would weigh them with their hand, and which weighed heaviest they took for the best…" In this way the innocent birds could be slaughtered by the thousands in just a few hours. Cahows lay only one egg and this, combined with their ease of capture, almost led to their extinction, like the passenger pigeons of North America, who were unfortunate enough to become a business venture and were wiped out.

In less than a week after arriving on the island, Sir George Somers had some land near Gates' Bay cleared of knotweed and lilies, and vegetable seeds were planted that were salvaged from the *Sea Venture*. The lilies were not the species that have since made the island a sweet-smelling reputation—and a tidy profit—but were goat lilies, or goldenrod; so in addition to their other adjustments, some of the first settlers may have suffered the multiple miseries of hay fever, induced by these plants and by the cedar pollen.

The muskmelons, peas, onions, radishes, lettuce, kitchen herbs, and other English seeds failed, as the weather was hot and the season late. Bermuda's constant salt-laden breezes are no help to crops either. Much of the blame was unjustly put on the unfamiliar soil—that Devon-red earth that looks as if anything would flourish in it—and the average depth of island soil is a mere six inches, which discouraged generations of inhabitants from bothering to plow. Bermuda's first gardeners could not fail to notice, through one sense or another, the heaps of seaweed that floated from the Sargasso Sea, but if anyone suggested using it as fertilizer, it must have been vetoed as far too risky for those precious fledgling crops; it was not tried as compost until the middle of the eighteenth century.

The *Sea Venture's* wreck had ruined the bread supply, but palmetto berries made the people "careless almost of any bread with their meat… The head of the Palmetto tree is very good meat, either raw or sodden," and weighs about twenty pounds, and "is far better than any cabbage." It was not "so offensively thankful to the stomack" either. The unripe berries were said to taste like damsons, though the ripe ones were appreciated by both people and pigs. Later these sweet-toothed hogs were to destroy the first sugar cane crop, though subsequent crops did not fare much better, as they could not stand up to the winds. The versatile palmetto also provided fronds for roofing the first houses, though it was horribly inflammable, and pathetically inadequate in the hurricanes that smite the island every two or three years.

Every tool, sail, piece of furniture, wood, or rope that could imaginably come in handy had been rescued from the wreck, though it was futile to pretend there was to be any permanent home on Bermuda, however idyllic it seemed. There was no evading the fact that the castaways were duty-bound to move on to the colony in Virginia, and for that they would need a ship. Only a few weeks after their landing, Gates had an experienced Limehouse shipwright, named Richard Frobisher, begin work on an eighty-ton ship, called the *Deliverance*, in a bay that became known as "Frobisher's Buildings" Bay, now Buildings Bay. At the same time, Henry Ravens, Mate of the *Sea Venture*, set off in her longboat fitted with a deck made from the hatches of the mother ship, and with sails and oars. With him went seven volunteers, to fetch help from Jamestown, expecting to be back in Bermuda in a month. In September Strachey saw to the setting up of a lookout on Saint David's Head, with a beacon at night; but the eight brave rescuers never reached Jamestown, nor apparently anywhere else.

While Ravens was gone, Somers built a small boat and circled the island, making the map that would eventually reach England with Strachey's letter. When, after two months of watching, it was evident that Ravens was not coming back, the Admiral, on the main part of the island, instigated the construction of a thirty-ton pinnace, named the *Patience*, laboring on it himself every day. The *Deliverance* was made partly of wood from the *Sea Venture*, and partly from the local cedar, but the *Patience* was entirely of cedar, with just one bolt in her keel. The vessels' lower seams were "caulked with the remains of the useless cables, and a small amount of tar saved from the wreck," and stones, shells, and turtle oil secured the upper seams.

All of this shipbuilding involved a great deal of hard work that most of the settlers were not used to, and there was the warm, humid weather to endure as well. But the building of two vessels also resulted in a division of loyalties, and meant that the people were not any too sure just whose orders they were supposed to be obeying. The two knights had had "a dispute about rank" even before they left England, and though the voyagers felt the greatest admiration for Somers in their shared ordeal of the storm, a beached Admiral was not as impressive as one at sea. In fact, while on board, he was said to be so passionate that few could please him, but yet ashore few could anger him. And as for Gates, even if he was the intended Lieutenant Governor of Virginia, what did that make him here in Bermuda?

Six recalcitrant fellows, with the religious fanatics among them proving the most tiresome, wanted work stopped on both vessels, and a self-governing society set up on Bermuda, where the climate was so relaxing and where the food seemed so plentiful. Gates demonstrated his qualities of governorship by sending the lot of them off to a small, distant island where they would have to manage entirely on their own, and could see how well they liked that idea when it became a reality. They didn't enthuse over the arrangement for long, and when they came back, Gates forgave them.

This leniency meant that another commotion soon occurred, when a well-educated man named Stephen Hopkins wanted to stay on in Bermuda too. After a formal trial Gates ordered him to be shot, but Hopkins made such an eloquent appeal on behalf of his wife and children that he won over "the hearts of all the better sort of the company," who persuaded Gates to relent once more. (Hopkins eventually returned to England and then went off in the *Mayflower* in 1620 to help colonize New England, and a descendant of *his* became a prolific writer of sea tales).

Very shortly a third mutiny arose, in which a group planned to murder Gates and his supporters, seize food and supplies, and set up their own government. In mid-March the leader, Henry Paine, confessed after a trial and was sentenced to be hanged that same day. Upon Paine pointing out that since he was a gentleman, it would be more fitting if he were shot, he was dispatched at sundown by his preferred method.

This sobered the rebels, who fled into the undergrowth, then asked Gates for a year's supply of food and clothing, so that they could stay behind on the island.

He flatly refused, as he was obliged to the investors to deliver the colonists to Virginia; apparently Somers was enamored of the island, however, and understood the insubordinates' feelings very well.

The time drew near when they must leave. Gates set up a memorial in Somers' garden in gratitude for their deliverance. A sea wall of rocks was made to facilitate embarkation; final work was completed on the two ships; they were loaded with supplies; and on May 12, 1610 the reluctant voyagers "were with difficulty prevailed upon to quit these pleasant islands." During the nine months' stay one marriage had been celebrated and two babies had been born: a girl named Bermuda, who was Strachey's goddaughter, and died on the island shortly afterwards, and a boy named Bermudas. Bermuda's father was John Rolfe, who would take for his second wife the Princess Pocahontas, and would find out how to cure Virginia tobacco to make it palatable to the English.

Not quite a full complement of passengers and crew showed up, however, on that May morning to depart in the *Deliverance* and the *Patience*. Ravens and his mates were missing. Five people had died, and two of the rebels were found to be mysteriously absent, having good reason to suppose they would be met in Jamestown with a noose, because of other serious offences they had committed. One man was Robert Waters, who had killed another sailor by hitting him under the ear with a shovel. The other was Christopher Carter.

Also missing was Namuntuck, who had been done in by Matchumps, after an argument, These two Indians had been sent to England, as a publicity stunt, by colorful Captain John Smith, who was in charge of the Virginia

Colony, and they had been on their way home in the *Sea Venture*. Matchumps, like many another murderer, had a disposal problem. He found he had dug too short a hole, and had to lay Namuntuck's legs—after separating them from their trunk—alongside the corpse. (He kept quiet about the entire episode until he got to Virginia).

Arriving safely at Jamestown on May 23, the transient Bermudians had "but a mournful welcome" from the handful of sixty starving, mutinous survivors. Colonial America and the West Indies provided splendid places to ship troublemakers, and the breeding propensities of unsavory characters were as good as anyone else's. This disastrous collection "consisted of unruly sparks, packed off by their friends, to escape a worse destiny at home…and of poor gentlemen, poor tradesmen, rakes and libertines, footmen, and such others as were much fitter to ruin a commonwealth than to help raise or maintain one." Because of the loss of the *Sea Venture* the previous year, the food shortage had been desperate, and an air of utter hopelessness hung over the whole place. There were many happy reunions between the *Sea Venture* people and others from the original fleet who had reached Virginia the year before, living through both the hurricane and the "starving time"— among them was Somers' nephew Matthew—but there must have been a lot of wishing to turn round and sail straight back to Bermuda. Of Ravens they could learn nothing, though there were rumors that he and the other seven men had reached another part of the Virginia coast, and had been taken prisoner by savages.

Admiral Somers availed himself of his rank and "cheerfully offered" to go back to the islands to fetch supplies for Virginia. Setting sail some weeks later in the *Patience*, with Matthew Somers as Captain, he finally reached Bermuda, "after long struggling with contrary winds." Officially, his mission was to catch and salt hogs and fish, but he was determined to see the island again, and may have had some understanding with Carter and Waters as well. Finding them healthy and content, Somers decided that a future Bermuda colony was an excellent idea, and that he would contribute some of his own money, if need be, to the financing of it.

The company from the *Patience* gradually began to accumulate provisions to take back to Virginia (gradually, because it wasn't easy to find time for all that catching and salting in such seductive surroundings). But regrettably all these exertions proved "too severe for his advanced age"— he was fifty-six—and the Admiral died on November 9, 1610. (A chronicle written in 1631 ascribes his death to "a surfeit of eating a pig" rather than to overwork). The dying Somers begged his men to bury him on island soil, and to return to Virginia, but both of this honorable man's requests were ignored. Instead of taking the desperately needed supplies to Virginia, Matthew went home to England, with his uncle's embalmed body in a cedar box, for burial in Dorset. Matthew squandered his share of the Admiral's estate and ended his days in jail. But Sir George's heart was buried on the island (along with his less romantic innards); so in essence that wish was carried out, and he became just the first of thousands of people who were to leave their hearts in Bermuda.

Christopher Carter was positive he wanted to stay behind once more, so Waters did too, and Edward Chard, the Admiral's servant. Expecting that a plantation would soon be established in the newly named Somers' Isles, they were now upgraded as personages holding the island for England. Watching the *Patience* sail away the three men must have anticipated only an interval of a few months on their own, but as it turned out they would be by themselves for close on two years.

Later generations of Bermudians have despised working on the land, as they considered it "positively degrading" and definitely preferred to make their living from the much more challenging sea; but they have benefited from the labors of these three sailors, who got down to it and cleared more land, on Smith's Island, and achieved splendid crops of beans, pumpkins, maize, melons, tobacco, and "many other good things for the use of man." They built more cabins and at least one boat. They cured bacon, trapped turtles, made salt from sea water, and searched for useful materials on the beaches.

Regrettably, Chard found, with other smaller lumps, the "greatest peece of Amber-Grece that the world is knowen ever yet to have had in one lumpe." This 80 per cent cholesterol substance may be made by sick whales, or by healthy ones to protect their intestines from the beaks of squid, and other sharp creatures that they eat. Chard's piece of ambergris was one of the largest on record, as it weighed at least eighty pounds and was worth a fortune. This was bound to put an unbearable strain on the relationship among the three men. They hid the treasure, but as each of them coveted it, they fought violently, bashing at each other with oars; and in this tragicomic battle the dog of one of them even bit his master. Chard and Waters decided to settle it with an official duel, but Carter, scared of being left all alone on the island, hid their swords. Then, with their mutual dependence staring them in the

face, they all quieted down and planned to build a pinnace in which to get away to Newfoundland, hoping to go from there to England with the fishing boats, and reap a shared reward from their ambergris.

However, they hadn't got very far with the boatbuilding when, at last, on July 11, 1612 they saw a ship anchor off Smith's Island. It was the *Plough*, carrying fifty or sixty people to be Bermuda's first official colonists, and their Governor, Richard Moore. The island's three caretakers soon tried to arrange with the *Plough*'s skipper for him to take their treasure back to England secretly; but then Carter thought better of this and told Moore. However, this confidence misfired, as Moore promptly appropriated the ambergris and put Chard in prison. Carter and Waters got away with a rebuke. Later on Moore sent the ambergris to England, little by little, in the supply ship that put in once or twice a year, so as to gratify and stimulate the gentlemen of the Virginia Company.

Bermuda's first governor was a carpenter—governors' vocations have changed a bit since then—and a contemporary described him as "an excellent artist, a good gunner, very witty and industrious." He was also courageous, fairminded, and canny. He needed all of these attributes, since being responsible for a brand new colony was uphill work. Moore was not confronted by the difficulty of making friends with Indians, nor with combatting wild animals or bitter cold, but he was expected to keep his people fed and content—and working, in a climate that continuously invites the laborer to put down his tools and sit in the shade of a flowering tree. As the solitary figure in command, and so very remote from higher authority to back him up, Moore was well aware that he must be firm, whether his people liked him or not.

Governor Moore set up his new administration on Smith's Island, then moved across the harbor to St. George's. He built a church, and a "palace" that served for many of his successors, though it had become pretty leaky by the turn of the eighteenth century. On Smith's Island, with its 61 acres, he supervised experimental plantings of eighty-one varieties of seeds, faithfully carrying out the instructions he had been given for the care of soil and vegetation. (A tropical textbook followed in Governor Butler's time). Moore also had complete directions for looking after the many nets which he had brought in the *Plough*. They were to be hung up to dry thoroughly; they must be mended properly, protected from rain, from sharp surfaces, and from mice. If plenty of time was given to their care, they might last four years. Otherwise, neglected nets, lines and boats would render the community destitute, which is just what did happen under the next governor, Daniel Tucker, the forceful Virginia planter who is immortalized in the American folk song, "Ol' Dan Tucker." Finding the island extremely short of food, he made the islanders set to and work hard at agriculture, for which they despised him. Tucker's stringent rule was very good for the island, but his relationship with the islanders was far from compatible. However, he must have forgiven them, for he later returned to live, and end his days there.

The investors in England, who had never set foot on Bermuda, and did not care to hear about its drawbacks, cherished overblown notions of what the island could produce (partly because of the glowing reports spread by those who had gone back in the *Patience*), and they indulged in extravagant dreams of the fortunes they would realize from the island's ambergris, tobacco, pearls, and whale oil. The Virginia Company was not interested in hearing about Moore's problems; they just wanted a good return on their investments, and sent repeated complaints and unrealistic demands. But there was hardly any ambergris; there were few pearls; tobacco was most unresponsive to the island's soil; and whale oil was very hard to come by.

There were plenty of whales—in fact their seasonal friskings kept the Bermudians awake—but catching them was very dangerous and difficult, and the methods of the time particularly cruel and wasteful. Hunting whales continued off Bermuda until early in this century, although the islanders gradually lost interest in it, since the profits went to England. Anyway, oil, "sea beef," and whale skin were needed at home. Bermudians knew how to cook the choice head and shoulder cuts so that they tasted like veal. Oil was used for lamps until the end of the nineteenth century, when kerosene was introduced, and whale skin was used for shoes and some of the other items that landlubbers usually make from leather.

Moore, who hoped that somehow the island could become self-sustaining, worked the colonists hard. He not only had them fish, dig, and sow, but he felt they should build eight or nine forts as well. All but one were wooden. When he came out from England, rumors had been rife that the Spanish wanted Bermuda as a link in their empire; they would feel much better about carrying home their booty from the West Indies if the island belonged to them. They had an excellent spy system and when the Ambassador in London sent back word about the ambergris, Bermuda became even more desirable.

In March, 1614 two Spanish ships came to give Bermuda a closer inspection to ascertain how much fortification the colonists had erected. One of the ships and a boat came in nearer to shore, and two island launches went out to look them over. The Spaniards invited the Englishmen to come aboard to talk, but they refused and stayed within the range of their fort's guns. Then these guns fired at the Spanish, who thought it more prudent to go away again, not having any inkling that Moore's magazine now consisted of precisely one barrel of gunpowder which had been accidentally knocked over. It is quite possible that the Spanish were very low on ammunition themselves, for when two Spanish galleons met at sea they went through a ritual of exchanging salutes—the oceanic equivalent of bowing and scraping—which wasted precious ammunition that might later be desperately needed to fend off a pirate attack.

Moore's diversion of labor to the forts meant that agriculture was neglected, and the food supply became seriously inadequate. The Scottish minister, Keath, complained so vociferously and with such effect, that there was nearly a mutiny. But Moore made him apologize publicly, then imprisoned and tried the other chief troublemakers, sentencing them to be hanged, and then pardoned them—a little bit of theater that made them all glad to toe the line again.

Assuming from their endless complaints that the investors were displeased enough to recall him, Richard Moore sailed home before his three years were up, being only the first of many Bermuda governors who were disheartened by the job. But the Company members were rather surprised to see him, and after "much wrangling" treated him civilly and gave him eight shares of land as salary. Moore had arranged for six men to look after the island, taking turns for a month apiece, until his replacement arrived. Chard (released from jail), Carter, and Waters were among these ineffectual substitutes. The islanders had a great time, and turning their backs on work, became a pack of tosspots.

Subsequently Chard and Waters went to Virginia, and Carter was offered Saint David's Island in payment for having told about the ambergris; but he chose Cooper's Island instead because he understood there was treasure buried on it. He stayed in Bermuda for the rest of his life, but never found any fortune more substantial than the pleasure of living there.

Hamilton Harbour

Coral wall, Fairylands

Roadside

*Garage,
Malabar Road*

Poinsettia

Morning glory

Somerset

Albouys Point, Hamilton

Hydrant, Hamilton

Roofs and croton

Frangipani

North Shore

Garden, St. George's

Paradise down to earth

Bermuda, settled as a business investment, was supposed to operate at a profit, and each governor was sent there with this understanding. In 1614 the Virginia Company relinquished its claim to Bermuda and King James gave a separate charter to the Somers' Island Company the following year. Among other rights, the island could call a General Assembly empowered to make Bermudian laws, as long as they were not in conflict with those of England. The Somers Island Company was a kind of absentee committee, running Bermuda from London, choosing her governors and sending supplies. In return, it expected pearls, tobacco, silk, whale oil, and ambergris. But the Company was irked because these were not forthcoming in anything like the hoped-for quantities, and the Bermudians were disgruntled at the condescending attitude of the Company which managed their lives for 69 years. So they petitioned the king—now Charles II—for a remedy, and finally in 1684 the Company forfeited its charter to the Crown, which took Bermuda under its rule and chose the governors. However, the island still had the right to make its own laws, and it was not a Crown colony.

After Richard Moore went back to England the governors varied, but were mostly a firm lot. Some of them overdid it a bit and soon found the 'Mudians were self-assertive, stubborn, and opinionated. This must have had something to do with their English ancestry. They were insular (many of them still don't think that much of the world outside, and have a point); they were sure they were right; and they probably thought their orneriness was a justifiable form of self-preservation.

Economic self-sufficiency was a nagging problem right from the start. During the first ten years tobacco, plantains, potatoes, grapes, fennel, basil, indigo, soapberries, cotton, figs, hemp, apricots, pineapples, and cassava were tried;

and goats, cattle and bees from the animal kingdom. Through the years the population occasionally declined because of a particularly large number of shipwrecks (in 1722 there were three women to each man), or because of yellow fever, but on the whole the inhabitants increased steadily, and some kind of produce had to be found to send off-island to pay for food, clothing, and the other necessities that must be brought in.

The first export was tobacco, though the Bermudians, of all ages and sexes, smoked and chewed a prodigious amount themselves. However, it was so "base" that eight inspectors (one for each tribe, or parish) were sent out by Charles I in 1626 to see what ailed the plant. These Tryers and Tasters improved the quality of the crop after experimenting for a while, though until 1630 it was described as "fit only for Dutchmen to smoke." But even their expertise couldn't make tobacco profitable and various other crops were attempted on and off for years. Olives, castor-oil plants, flax, sisal and aloes were all grown with varying degrees of unsuccess.

Gradually domestic animals were brought from England and the West Indies; but some were just an annoyance. Errant turkeys took a heavy toll of the corn and onions, and some of them ended up accidentally-on-purpose as roasts and feather dusters at the neighbors'. Rabbits were introduced and, though very acceptable fare to seventeenth-century Englishmen, are considered not much better than vermin by modern Bermudians.

As well as the pests and diseases that afflicted plants there was a considerable number for humans. There were cholera, smallpox, yellow fever, and dengue or breakbone fever, distemper, typhus, tuberculosis, measles, and a few cases of leprosy. Among a choice of persistent aggravations were chiggers, which laid their eggs between the toes of anyone who went barefoot.

One of the island's more dramatic curses was "a wonderful annoyance of filly Rattes" sent from above to punish the current pharoah, Daniel Tucker, for his severity. Spawned by rats that had arrived in a load of meal during Richard Moore's time, they resisted poison, dogs, traps, a special consignment of fierce English cats, and even extensive burning of the cedar trees. But providence relented, and sent a deluge that did the trick; the rats were flushed out in a few days. (Perhaps it was like the storm of 1902 which in two hours achieved twelve feet of water in the vegetable garden of Admiralty House).

The early houses were made of wood and palmetto, but as they didn't survive very well, in 1703 it was required that buildings be made of stone, for resistance to rain and hurricanes. Two-handled saws were used to cut limestone blocks from the ground, and early quarries were near the water so that the stone could be more easily transferred about the island. Houses too were placed near water, for accessibility to the obvious means of transportation. Later on, for even greater feasibility, blocks were hewn out beside where a house was to be built, leaving space all ready to be made into a sunken garden, or terrace.

Today the limestone is harder to reach, and consequently more expensive, so cement blocks are widely used instead. But when they have been color-washed there is little difference to the eye.

At first the heavy hauling was done by men; later horses were brought in, though they were taxed for fear they would eat more feed than could be spared. Both horses and cattle were moved, when necessary, by making them swim from one island to the next. Rowboats were the equivalent of today's family car, for shorter trips, and

people managed to look dignified, even in their social finery, just as their descendants looked quite proper all dressed up on bicycles.

With horses on the island getting about was easier, though travel was on horseback—a sign of gentility—as roads were too rough and narrow for vehicles until the mid-nineteenth century. (Tribe roads, wide enough for a horse and for rolling a barrel along, are, thank goodness, still inaccessible to cars). Even when streets were widened, most people continued to ride, as carriages were a bit swanky and too expensive, since they involved more harness, and the upkeep of the tack and the vehicle. Governor Alured Popple brought the first sedan chair in 1738, but they were unsuitable outside town, so women rode a horse, alone or on a pillion. White girls riding to a ball were accompanied by a black servant carrying a trunk with the dress and other necessities. Country roads were pitch dark except when the moon shone, but in town people carried torches of rolled palmetto; though there was such a fear of fire that it was illegal for servants to carry them. If they were caught doing so, they were whipped.

Servants ran most of the errands, but the master of the house usually did the marketing on a Saturday, which gave him a chance to hob-nob with his friends and to assimilate liquor with the weekly news. Wives would have liked to go along too, but it wasn't considered correct. However, by the turn of the twentieth century husbands were beginning to allow this freedom.

Expecting their gardens and the sea to provide most of their wants, few households bought much besides a few staples. For shopping, householders took their own bags, jugs, or tins with them. Some used a holdall bag, and care in packing and unpacking it was essential. Split peas, corn, sugar, or whatever were put in the bag, one category at a time, with a string tied tightly between each. Then at home each 'waist' was untied and the contents of the section poured out. As coopering was a local industry, field produce was transported in potato or flour barrels sawn in half, with rope handles fitted on.

Since World War II it has become "square" to be frugal and re-use containers. Sad to say, Mark Twain's "the tidiest place in the world" is no longer so, as the trash wave has hit Bermuda, though in a milder form. Seductive packaging has developed into an art form taken very seriously by its promoters, and modern society uses a proliferation of bottles, cans, paper, and wrappings, but loses interest in them as soon as they have done their job. Out they go, to catch in hedges, float on the breeze, or on the water and then to wash up on the beaches. Plastic that cracks so readily and becomes useless for its intended purpose, is perverse enough to remain inde-structible after it has been thrown away. The new Bermuda has not only her own rubbish disposal eyesore, in the lesser-seen streets and coves, but even collects residue tossed overboard in the Sargasso Sea. (The island also has the sad distinction of receiving forty times more beach tar than the coast of Florida, between Miami and Palm Beach).

"Remote" is one of the very favorite words of writers, when on the subject of Bermuda. Sitting out there by herself, she has always been acutely aware of her economic dependence on England and the American mainland. But her very isolation and smallness developed a determination to "do it myself" and if one means of support was a failure, she tried another. Bermudians had built hundreds of sea-going and fishing boats before the end of the seventeenth century, and the number increased annually until the American Revolution was over; but there was a gradual change from other land-based occupations to the sea in the eighteenth century, which meant less and less food grown at home, and increasing dependence on imports. Bermudians had always fished (though that breeze that makes the island habitable in hot weather was often strong enough to prevent fishing boats from putting out), and there were few men competent in any other skill; though there were silverworkers on the island throughout the nineteenth century, using seventeenth century silver that came with the early settlers, and material gleaned from Spanish wrecks.

Bermuda men expertly sailed their durable, swift, highly-prized cedar vessels, "the best in the world," taking whatever produce they could muster, or domestic fowls, or perhaps ballast of local limestone, to trade with in the Caribbean Islands. Sometimes passengers, or rum, tea, calico, and sugar were taken from the West Indies to England; or goods were exchanged in the Canaries with ships arriving from China or India. From the late eighteenth to the mid-nineteenth century Bermuda's carrying trade was out of all proportion to her size, and fortunes were made that enabled local families to be held in high esteem for generations.

For nearly a hundred years salt from the Caribbean was the biggest standby. Beginning in 1678, most of it came from Turk's Island, the small easternmost link of the Bahamas chain, nearly a thousand miles south of Bermuda. Some years as many as 2000 men were employed. Part of the Bermudian crews were put off on Turk's while they evaporated and raked the dazzling salt in the tropical sun for months at a time. Then the men and the salt were picked up by returning Bermudians who had been trading in turtles, treasure, and tall tales in other parts of the Caribbean, and taken back to Bermuda. When good weather came the salt was taken to seaboard ports in North America, where it was bartered for pine, codfish, flour, and other commodities that the islanders were gasping for. By 1750 approximately one-tenth of the population was engaged in the salt business, and 100,000 bushels of it were traded each year.

Bermuda men might be found on any of the seas, even though conditions afloat were so bad that it was said a man who went to sea for pleasure would go to hell for a pastime. But colonial seamen used all their guile to avoid being sent to England, as they had heard about the horrors of being press-ganged into the navy during the wars that cropped up intermittently in Europe, America, and the West Indies. The Bermuda sailors were welcomed everywhere as newsbearers, and they brought shells, curios, "intelligence" (gossip), and plants home to their tiny island.

Bermudians had always found agriculture a deadly bore, and claiming it couldn't be done because of the shape of the island, or because of the soil, they managed to be noticeably inefficient at the work. But horticulture was very satisfying to them. Cuttings from new additions were eagerly exchanged, and at present there are over 950 different kinds of trees and plants to enjoy, though less than two dozen of them are indigenous. Practical uses were soon found for some of the newcomers. The oleander, arriving in 1790, was planted to form boundaries and wind breaks; a stick of it with leaves on the end made a ceiling duster, and leaf chains were good for church decorations. The sticks made good lining-hoops for barrels, as well.

All this sounds very domestic and mild, but there had to be a rougher side to Bermudians' personalities. For a considerable time wrecking was a life-saver—at any rate for the islanders. Being so dependent on outside supplies, they could not be expected to keep their hands off the well-laden ships that foundered on the rocks, or to let the contents float about and get smashed on the island's doorstep. But politely waiting for natural shipwrecks would hardly have borne enough fruit, and the same spirit prevailed as in Cornwall, where they used bonfires and false lanterns—a horn beacon was a lamp hung on a cow's horns as she innocently wandered about on a cliff top. Correctly placed lanterns often suffered from a puzzling shortage of oil just when they were most needed, and the Cornish wreckers "with lanterns, carts, crowbars, wheel-barrows and sacks…waited on shore" with mounting excitement and gleeful anticipation.

Before the Merchant Shipping Act of 1876 there was no Plimsoll mark to indicate the maximum load line—it wasn't adopted internationally until 1930. Tremendous numbers of ships were sent out with rotten timbers and far too much cargo, and were overinsured by owners who callously hoped they would become floating coffins. The skimpy crews, kept in line by masters with relentless discipline, were underpaid, underfed, and unwilling, and were likely to mutiny at the first chance they could seize. In Bermuda, when a distressed ship—"a turtle in the net" —was seen to have struck the reefs, the islanders went out in gigs and whaleboats to welcome it into their predacious clutches, and to relieve it of its cargo. In its earlier days Bermuda was known to have natives who were gentle and affectionate, but "the privilege of fishing for wrecks" was something else, and victimized ships' crews were sometimes astonished to witness the greed with which the Bermudians cut down and hauled away rigging, ripped down sails, and pounced on cargo, so that local stomachs could be comforted and homes embellished with the proceeds.

There was a pervasive atmosphere of violence and cruelty throughout the Caribbean for many years, and it was inevitable that Bermuda should join in the lucrative trades of privateering and piracy, which sometimes had a rather fine line between them. In the seventeenth and eighteenth centuries the island itself was sacked over thirty times by pirates, who had a "longing eye after these Islands." Life was held very cheap, and pirate lords devised sickening and ingenious ways of making their captives, some of whom were Bermudians, tell where treasure was hidden. Men, women, and children were all treated alike, and suffered so much they could scarcely have thought clearly enough to reveal anything, even if they did know the answer. But as governments and crowns are very interested in getting their share of the loot, crime often pays, and even treacherous, sadistic Henry Morgan was rewarded by Charles II with a knighthood and the lieutenant governorship of Jamaica.

Before the discovery of the New World, Europe looked in an easterly direction for the mythical pot of gold, but after the addition of a huge new area to plunder, the gold rush swung westward. Trade was established between England and the West Indies, where besides other commodities vital to the developing empire, were the dyestuffs for England's flourishing wool trade. But pirates were "so numbrous" by Queen Anne's reign that they almost brought the trade to a standstill with their outrageous plunder. Parliament dragged its feet, and it wasn't until George I's reign that the Royal Navy was sent to patrol the West Indies and to "annoy" the pirates. However, the Navy's warships were so ponderous that the nimbler pirate ships ran circles round them, and just went on controlling the Spanish Main—a circuit of about 12,000 miles. It was the Navy that was annoyed instead.

The headquarters and training school of the pirate settlement was at New Providence (now Nassau), with its excellent harbor and permanent population of traders and hangers-on, living in makeshift palm-leaf dwellings and tents. A plentiful supply of liquor and dissolute women made the area very attractive to roving, lawless men. Mostly from the English seaport slums, many of them had been orphans or illegitimate waifs, who became voluntary sailors or enforced apprentices, and eventually pirates. After a war there were suddenly large numbers of unemployed seamen who were not interested in tame jobs, even if there were any to be had. Their ranks were augmented by ex-convicts sent to the colonies as indentured servants who, after their term was over, or if they had escaped, were destitute.

Not all convicts were villainous, as jail terms were handed out for many minor offenses. Indentured servants might be anything from intellectuals to pickpockets, as all species of undesirables were sold into bondage by their governments for three to seven years, though there was no guarantee of freedom at the end of the period. Tens of thousands of indentured servants were shipped across the sea and sold to work on plantations, many of them becoming the property of masters who indulged in unrestrained cruelty, if they felt inclined. Shocking deals to obtain these servants were set up by planters, captains, and go-betweens. Stolen children were trafficked in by the thousands, but preferably those over the age of eight, as younger ones usually died on the voyage. These people provided labor for the colonies for at least fifty years until blacks were kidnaped to take their place. Although never referred to as slaves, they often received worse treatment than the blacks, who were generally in a state of servitude for life and represented a bigger investment.

Bondsmen were expendable, since their term was up in a few years, and it mattered little whether they survived or not. If they did, or if they escaped, they faced only hardship and did better for themselves by disappearing into the anonymity and adventure of piracy.

Bermuda's governor called Nassau a "sink or nest of infamous rascals" but it was only natural that his island should join in the excitement and the gains. The import/export business became the life of Bermuda, and shops, taverns, and the sidelines all flourished. But Bermuda didn't fall as low as the Bahamas, even though her resources were as meager.

Conventional resources may have been in short supply, but the island's assured gifts to humanity were the climate, the quiet friendliness and courtesy of her people, and the beauty of her surroundings. The scenery is not to be described in grandiose terms, but it is softly insistent and accessible, and gives unfailing pleasure of some kind, at any time; while the climate, though not perfect, offers more than many other parts of the earth. So, gradually the island's reputation for being gentle, healthful, and welcoming, grew and spread.

In less than half a century after Bermuda's settlement, tourists began to arrive from New England, the West Indies, and Virginia. Refugees from the cold on the one hand, and from malaria-bearing mosquitoes on the other, they were at first the relatives and friends of island families. The journey by sail took weeks; and even much later, in the days of steamers, Mark Twain said "Bermuda is Paradise, but you have to go through Hell to get to it." No, getting there could never be said to be half the fun. But the modern visitor who goes by comfortable cruise ship, or by short plane flight, cannot imagine the surge of delight and relief with which the newly-arrived

passenger first saw the unspoilt islands in the (good) old days. At the end of the stay it must have been hard to face the return journey, but one early visitor faced it with strength he had never hoped to enjoy again. The Reverend Michael Wigglesworth, a "rhyming divine" from Malden, Massachusetts, went to Bermuda in 1663 in a state of very poor health and not really expecting to recover. The month-long passage nearly polished him off altogether, but a stay from October to May so set him up that he went home and took two additional wives—one at a time—fathered several more children, and fathered his parish as well for another forty years.

Hundreds of other writers have stayed in Bermuda: critics, editors, poets, playwrights, novelists, and scientific and suspense writers, from L. Frank Baum, author of *The Wizard of Oz*, and Du Bose Heyward, author of *Porgy and Bess*, to Mark Twain, Rudyard Kipling, Eugene O'Neill, and Lucius Beebe. Some of them found they could write while there just because of the unobtrusiveness of the scenery, while others, finding work impossible, just soaked up the atmosphere and relaxed. And told themselves they would work all the better for it when they got home. The early visitors went on "rambles," and if they overdid it, tired feet responded to a soak in seawater. They went to amateur performances of music, drama and dance (now there are world-renowned artists and festivals); they went to foot races, rowing races, and horse races; or they slept, or watched the world go by. (Bermudians have always been wall-sitters, which is not at all the same as fence-sitters). Very little world did go by, before the importation of cars in 1946. In Word War II jeeps and trucks tore about, raising clouds of white dust, which defenseless bicyclists choked down as part of their war effort, but it was quite possible to sit by the road for an hour and see no traffic pass.

Besides writers, artists, titles, politicians, and "personalities" (their chief claim to fame), the island has welcomed masses of ordinary mortals—but once they are in their bathing suits the names and the nobodies are indistinguishable. They all come to shed their responsibilities for a while, and to enjoy the clean air, the quiet, the flowers, the flash and song of birds, the orderly way of life, and the warmth of sun and hospitality. And they come to walk on the beaches and to slosh in the sea; the idea of marinas, private beaches, and heated pools gobbling up so many gardens, would once have seemed incongruous, but it's useless to resent the new facts of life.

Those who can, go to Bermuda with their loves. According to a recent brides' magazine survey, honeymooners comprise 20 per cent of the island's tourist visitors, and it's highest on the list of most popular places in which to start out on a new marriage (whether the first, second, or unspecified). A follow-up survey should be taken to find out the current status of those marriages; although Bermuda offers no guarantee of matrimonial endurance, the chances must be excellent. Lovers are like dolphins—perpetually receptive to opportunities for sensual enjoyment—and they have come to the right place.

Some visitors have to be more purposeful, as they have a job to do and are admitted into the ranks of temporary residents. Anthony Trollope visited for two weeks in the autumn of 1858 as inspector of West Indian post office systems, but the south wind blew the whole time, causing damp clothing and sticky hair. He was displeased by the irritability of everyone, especially of himself, and was overwhelmed by such a lassitude that he feared he had a fever, until the equally lethargic inhabitants assured him that the sensation was normal.

Tom Moore was probably the bounciest literary visitor the island has had. He was "a little man, but full of spirits, with eyes, hands, feet, and frame forever in motion... neat made and tidily buttoned up, young as fifteen at heart, though with hair that reminded me of Alps in sunset." (Another admirer said his hair was the color of a sovereign). Everyone was fond of him and he seems to have had more than his share of irresistible charm, even for an Irishman, although all his life he was surprised to find that people liked him. At twenty-four he was sent as Registrar of the Vice-Admiralty Court in Bermuda, as England was at war with Napoleon.

Moore left Portsmouth, in Hampshire, in September, 1803, but had a long delay in Virginia. His sentimental songs were already known there, and he captivated his listeners by singing the haunting melodies in his mellifluous voice. The British Consul's wife wept over him when he left Norfolk in January, 1804, in a Bermuda-built cedar sloop of war, and he reached Bermuda safely after seven days of horrible weather.

Living in St. George's, Moore enjoyed himself thoroughly with the 'Bermoodians,' as he claimed they called themselves. He rode over the winding lanes "through a thick shaded alley of orange trees and cedars, which opened now and then upon the lovliest coloured sea you can imagine, studded with little woody islands, and all in animation with sail boats." To console his mother for being so far away he wrote to tell her that Bermuda is "a place where physicians order their patients when no other will keep them alive." He thought the men of the island not very civilized, but the women, though not generally handsome, had an affectionate languor, "which is always interesting... a predisposition to loving... diffuses itself through the general manner." He dallied amorously with the ladies, and his famous poems to Nea were later much admired by the Shelleys. But the Edinburgh Review was devastating—"polluting...immoral ...ludicrous..." and Moore nearly fought a duel with the editor over this review. He had hoped to make the island a home for himself and his family, but it was soon evident that it was just no good as far as the job was concerned, because so many prize-courts had been established and so few cases were referred to the one in Bermuda, that there was no prospect of high fees. So he left toward the end of April, 1804, giving the reason as "a disorder in the chest," wherein lies the heart after all. But he told his mother that he was bringing home a sunburnt face and a heart not the worse for wear.

Leaving a local deputy in Bermuda, Moore traveled four hectic months in America and Canada, then went back home with a completed volume of poems. His appointment was not cancelled until 1844. The American War of 1812-1815 should have given him a financial boost, but the deputy sent him nothing and absconded in 1818, saddling the poet with the obligation of several thousand pounds, which he couldn't possibly meet. He was forced to live in Europe from 1819 to 1822 to escape imprisonment for debt, but the episode was ultimately settled, though it cost Moore plenty of money and considerable anxiety. He was a prolific poet, though his letters are more digestible than his saccharine verse, and he did capture the atmosphere of Bermuda as few other poets have done.

Edmund Waller and Andrew Marvell never went to the island, but wrote about it anyway, which in that respect alone puts them on the same shelf as Shakespeare. They rhapsodized about the resources and languorous atmosphere, and Marvell made the mistake of describing the climate as being like a perpetual spring, whereas the variance in behavior is part of the appeal of Bermuda weather. They hadn't a clue either about the tense, keyed-up feeling that comes before a hurricane, or the exciting smell of broken vegetation afterwards.

In 1616 the English-speaking world lost its greatest playwright, while across the Atlantic the small new colony gained some startling new color. The *Edwin* came from the West Indies with an Indian and a black who were indentured servants, as were most of the first black workers. The next governor, Nathaniel Butler, sent to the West Indies for blacks skilled in pearl diving and sugar cane growing, as they were "the most proper and cheap instruments." The majority of blacks were brought from the West Indies or had been seized from the Spanish or Portuguese. White people were totally ignorant of the slaves' African or Indian heritage, and insensible to the concept of them as people basically like themselves. They simply thought of them as savages whom they could work and chastise with a clear conscience, since they were not Christians, and had "not a right to the same liberty of trial as the English men."

From then on, a very large part of the colony's manual labor was done by blacks, and they featured prominently in Bermuda life, both ashore and at sea, even though most of the early censuses did not include them. Not all slaves were black, however. When Oliver Cromwell put the defenders of Drogheda to the sword in 1649, some of the few score survivors were shipped to plantations in Barbados, and some of them ended up in Bermuda.

Blacks, and some of the poor whites, built and white-washed houses, fences, and walls. They mended roads as well as the bridges which needed frequent repairs because of the hurricanes that hit every few years. Most dock-

Schoolgirls, St. George's

Natural Arches,
Tuckers' Town

*Soncy Cottage,
Fairylands*

Caddy, Castle Harbour Golf Course

Young
Bermudian

Somerset

Honeymooners

View, Hamilton

Magazine,
Dockyard

Near
Horseshoe

Lizard

t Street, Hamilton

Government Hill Road, St. George's

John Smith's Bay

From Gibbs' Hill Lighthouse

St. Anne's Church, Southampton: detail

Wall, St. George's

Bougainvillaea and elephant ears

Hamilton Harbour

Paget

Cottage

Spanish Bayonet

64   *Palm and wall*

CEDAR AVENUE

St. Theresa's Cathedral, Hamilton

Roofline, North Shore

Roof, from St. David's Lighthouse

Botanical Gardens

Cedar, 1943

*Lighthouse
Gibbs' Hill*

Constables, Hamilton

Marsden Methodist Church

St. James' Church, Sandys Parish

On Pitt's Bay Road

*St. Mark's cemeta
Smith's Parish*

Natural Arc
Tucker's To

In Hamilton

Ferry captain

workers were black, with the added advantage of being hard to spot when loading and unloading contraband. Blacks ran errands, did the shopping, carried water, made shoes, got rid of pests, were dressmakers, maids, valets, and cooks—and like most cooks were in an enviable position for pilfering extra food for their families. Blacks cared for white children too—their own were looked after by older slaves, to leave the parents free for work. In the West Indies, with its large plantations, one person was likely to own hundreds of slaves, but in Bermuda few owned as many as thirty, though some landowners had more than they needed or could afford. The notion of selling familiar servants was hateful, and owning plenty was prestigious.

Bermudians were renowned for their seamanship—blacks and whites equally. Other crews dreaded encountering the black ones at sea, as sometimes they vented their frustrations by running wild, and their officers were unable to control them. By the beginning of the eighteenth century the island had 170 pilots, who were predominantly black or Indian. The job required strong nerves and keen eyesight, and the Bermudians were remarkably skillful at it. Because of this, islanders feared that pirates or the Spanish might capture a pilot and be able to get into Bermuda's excellent but difficult harbors. The competition was fierce for piloting jobs, as fees were divided between the pilot and crew. Lookouts were perched in cedars on the best hills, to watch for approaching sails, and when a ship was spotted, there was a scramble for the gigs in which pilots were taken out. Gigs were from 32 to 42 feet long. Manned by six or eight oars and with two or three sails, they made up to 14 knots, and might travel fifty miles from land, as each team was determined to be first to reach the incoming vessel. But however competitive the

teams were, it was understood that the first pilot to hail the ship and climb aboard earned the job of bringing her in.

In the colony's early days manual skills were greatly in demand and men were paid in pounds of tobacco, according to their skill. Laborers got one pound a day, the highest paid being sawyers who got 3 pounds. Tobacco purchased other kinds of labor too. There was a shortage of white girls for the white men to marry. So, as with other urgently desired commodities, they were brought over from England and sold to any man who could pay 100 pounds of tobacco. They were snapped up and the shortage persisted, so black women became very acceptable substitutes and had even less choice in the matter than the white ones. The island's first mixed marriage was in 1633. One of the Indian women who had gone to England with Pocahontas was married in St. George's to a very amiable gentleman there, and more than a hundred guests attended.

Besides weddings and funerals to break the monotony, there were frequent slave balls, which were astonishingly lavish and colorful affairs that gave the participants a rare opportunity for dressing up in finery that they were not even supposed to possess. But with so many of their men going to sea and surreptitiously bringing back materials, trinkets, buttons, and buckles from other ports, the black women made themselves beautiful dresses, and in the latest styles. As they were continually having it impressed on them it was better to be white, the blacks did their best to come up to, and surpass, the clothes of the white women on these occasions. The whites marveled at the "extraordinary exertions" of the blacks, who danced far into the night, even in hot weather, wasting useful energy that would have been much better saved for the next day's work. The bands, composed of fiddles,

Spearfishing, South Shore

flutes and drums, were so noisy that the whites lost as much sleep as the dancers, but got none of the fun out of it. These balls were highly formal and "in short everything was conducted with the same taste as in the higher circles of society. They had Spanish dances and quadrilles, country dancing not being considered genteel." Tribal and folk dances were represented at Christmas time by the elaborately dressed Gombey dancers, as they still are today. "Gombey" comes from the African name of their drum, and as well as the original African influence, the dances have assimilated touches from Britain and from American and West Indians.

For supper at the slave balls there was an abundance of cakes, preserves, fowls, turkeys, and brandy and other liquors. Respectable white women did not attend, as it would have been indiscreet, though they must have been devilishly curious about these dances; but the white men did. The dance floor was a more neutral ground where the master-slave relationship could be relaxed a bit, and the white men were able to find a good selection of women from whom to pick out their mistresses.

The colonists were already frightened by the blacks' fertility before the end of the seventeenth century, but preferred to overlook the fact that miscegenation had quite a bit to do with it. Sex between whites and blacks was forbidden in 1663, because there were so many mulattoes; mixed marriages were outlawed in 1668 and further importation of slaves was banned in 1675 (though more were smuggled in). Of course, relationships went on just the same. Interbreeding was a two-way street, but it was usually the woman, of either color, who was most likely to be whipped for it. Midwives were pressured, before the birth of a baby, to discover and reveal the identity of the father.

The majority of writers on Bermuda have tip-toed round the concrete facts of intimate relationships between blacks and whites and of the measures taken by whites in the past to restrain and punish blacks. There were "blacks" with blue eyes soon after the colony began. There still are, and it has been convenient to attribute this feature—as inescapable as a dark skin—to the Scottish prisoners taken at Dunbar and Worcester by Cromwell in the English Civil War, who were brought to Bermuda in 1650 and 1651. Isn't there hope that by now, so long after Emancipation Day, modern "interracial" relationships can be acceptable to both sides without resentment or criticism, and given the privacy they deserve? As to punishment, perhaps it has been glossed over, and the emphasis put on some Bermudians treating their slaves almost like family, because of embarrassment and reluctance to admit that, due to fear and the ignorance of the times, so much unfeeling treatment was meted out to fellow humans.

The children of slaves were the property of the owner for a specified number of years, whoever the father was; and there were multiple and encompassing rules and regulations for the actions, possessions (or lack of them), destinies and punishments of servants. Thirty-nine lashes on the bare back was a sentence specially favored by the authorities, and it was doled out for circulating false rumors, or petitions for freedom for slaves; for bastardy; for buggery; for fornication; for selling rum or other liquors; and for cutting or injuring cedar trees. For rebellion 'R', for "rogue," was burnt into the forehead, the prisoner was whipped, and his nose was slit. After 1755, a black's ears were cut off for assaulting a white, and for killing one, the sentence was inevitably execution.

Sometimes this meant being burnt at the stake. Sally Bassett was burnt at the stake, one sweltering June day in

1730, at the foot of Crow Lane, having been convicted of trying to poison her master and mistress and a black girl by giving them ratsbane and manchineel root. Sally insisted she was innocent, right through the ordeal, and it was said that when her ashes were inspected later, a slender little purple flower was found among them. It was *Sisyrinchium bermudiana*, indigenous to the island, and perhaps it corroborated Sally's innocence.

Generally speaking, there was a double color standard all along the line. Certainly whites were flogged, or executed, but they were more likely to get off, and there is no record of a white having his body quartered, or suffering the agony and stigma of having his nose slit, nor the posthumous horror of having his severed head stuck up on a pole as a warning to passers-by. In 1704 the Assembly passed an act stating that blacks found guilty of insolence should be castrated; however, Whitehall, with the usual delay due to transportation, sent back a reprimand against such "inhumane penalties" and the act was repealed the next year.

It is clear that no matter how gruesome the punishments meted out to black and mulatto criminals and wrongdoers, they were ineffective as deterrents. There was such a desperation to escape that slaves took rash chances. Frequently they tried to run away, but it was a forlorn hope in such a place, and the punishment was severe. There were plots and plans for taking over the island, and many poisoning conspiracies. A number of whites had black food-tasters, but a lot of them died mysteriously anyway, some victims lingering for months. Other ways to escape white dominance were by inducing abortion, by murder, and by suicide. Some slaves were freed before their term was up, because of especially reliable behavior or some act of bravery, or devotion beyond mere duty. When

indentured servants became free, they could work and keep their wages and follow occupations not possible during their slavery, such as teaching, or renting rooms, though there were laws against owning property. The majority of slaves became free only through the wills of their owners or at the owners' deathbeds. Very few indeed could buy their own freedom, as there were scarcely any opportunities to accumulate money. At last the slavery system ended in all British colonies in 1834 and 4000 people in Bermuda were set free. The British Parliament provided compensation for slave owners—a transaction that took months to straighten out—and Bermuda and Antigua decided not to accept the apprenticeship clause but to allow their blacks to manage their own lives from then on, as some compensation for the two hundred years of restraint. However, Bermudians wasted no time in passing new legislation to ensure that the majority of blacks would be ineligible to vote or to run for most offices. Their chief stumbling block was illiteracy.

With the end of slavery, even less work was done in the fields, and there was a worse shortage of food. The palmetto had become so essential to the island that by the end of the eighteenth century it was protected by law, and once more it came to the rescue, this time providing income. Even former seamen made palmetto into elegant hats, shoes, purses, and trimmings for export. For domestic use they made bonnets, brooms, chairseats, workbaskets, ropes, fishpots, dolls and fans, and baskets for shipping vegetables off-island. Palmetto work was demoralizing for these previously active men, and yet others had the no more inspiring job of minding four blindfolded oxen that ground arrowroot, which was grown for some years at Camden, in Paget, and at St. David's and St. George's. The small wooden kegs for exporting the arrowroot were locally made as well. Until it was undersold and outproduced by larger places, Bermuda supplied arrowroot which, like the cedar ships and the men who sailed them, was "the best in the world."

Bermuda became steadily poorer, although she has never had any destitute, until yet another war rescued her from her quiet, insular life. The U.S. War of the North and South erupted in 1861 and the island hummed with hectic shipbuilding, blockade-running, and providing officers (at fat salaries) and crews for the Southern side—the Southern side because of blood connections and expediency. A sort of gold rush followed as get-rich-quick adventurers poured in from all round the world. Money and rum flowed freely; St. George's was full of wild fellows, and the town was neglected and vile. For four years the island was bursting with people, just as it would be again in World War II.

Lee surrendered; yet another slaughter had ended, and Bermuda was left to her old ways again. This time onions were the profitable crop and they were planted where the arrowroot had been before. In some areas even cedars were destroyed to make room for them. Potatoes and onions were exported to the northern United States until boxcars were refrigerated and American farmers could send vegetables to cities that used to buy them from Bermuda. Then customs duties went sky-high, and island farming nearly died out, except for its own use, though in hot weather it was just too much trouble and demanded more energy than Bermudians could muster for something they didn't want to do anyway. Meanwhile providence had been gradually working ro revive the island once more, and this time there was a peaceable solution.

As far as we can tell, nobody ever arrived in Bermuda by balloon. Jules Verne's Americans, who fled in one from Richmond, Virginia during the Civil War, ended up on a different volcanic isle in the Pacific. But some years earlier on an October day in 1833, hundreds of astonished Bermudians had lined up along the North Shore to watch another phenomenon—a steamer was approaching the island. The *Marco Bozzaris* was the first one the frightened inhabitants had ever seen, and as they waited to see what she would do, they never could have guessed that she was the harbinger of a whole new era of prosperity for them.

Soon steamers came twice a month to fetch produce for the New York market, and they brought a few visitors who had heard about the island's effect on jaded mainlanders. These people came to recuperate from illness, or to escape from the hurly-burly or the cold at home, and to seek a dream island where they could allow the slower pace to reach into them and soothe their jangling nerves. Mark Twain described the place as "tranquil and contenting," and having found such a refuge, he and many others returned again and again. There is a wistful island-lover in many of us—an island where we can cherish the illusions of private ownership and bask in the reality of seclusion and escape, and where we can pretend to be disassociated from all those (other) tourists.

Early visitors stayed with relatives or in private homes that had a spare room or two. Then hotels began to go up, staying open just from Christmas until Easter. The Hamilton Hotel, started before the Civil War, was finally finished; then the Hamilton Princess was built and named after Queen Victoria's daughter, Princess Louise, Duchess of Argyll, who rented Inglewood, in Paget, for her stay of several months of winter-dodging in 1883. Since then there has been built a superabundance of places to stay. Most of them nestle tactfully, but others poke up indecently, out of scale, and disappointingly reminiscent of all the tawdry

Cabanas and bay grape

Alley, St. George's

Golf Course, Castle Harbour

Early morning ferry

Royal palms

Wall, St. David's

St. Peter's Church, St. George's

Palmetto

Coral steps

St. George's

Bay grape

Farm

St. Peter's Church,
St. George's

101

102   *St. Mary's Church, Warwick*

Near Spanish Rock

high-rise that is so plentiful in the "real" world outside. Running short of space, Bermuda has begun to discard her sentimental, toy-village aspect for the sake of the expanding tourism that she needs; but it is to be hoped that the government will never forget that most visitors come back because they love the place the way it was last time, even if they cannot see it the way it was thirty years ago. Too bad that the most obtrusive building can't be folded up and stored away during all the weeks that it stands empty and redundant. In the real world we learn to accept tall buildings; the Eiffel Tower was built less than a century ago, in fields, and caused an uproar of indignation, yet now Paris cannot be imagined without it. The first Bermudiana Hotel, built in 1923 on a piece of "prime waterfront property," caused great dismay, but those of us who never saw Hamilton without it feel no shock. Yet even moderately tall buildings are just not appropriate in Bermuda, and we don't want to learn acceptance of them.

As the number of visitors increased annually, there were many more tastes to satisfy, and greater dependence on imported goods, though needs were simple for a time. Swiss watches, Waterford glass, and Danish swizzle sticks were not yet on merchants' invoices. However, there was the same old problem of disinclination for field work, especially now that there were good jobs in hotels and shops. (The notion that service equates with servility had not begun to filter in from the west). The visitors were saving the island from a slump, but who would save it from its own agricultural lethargy?

Before the Civil War there had been a small trickle of Portuguese immigrants and in the middle of the nineteenth century a great many more of these skillful, persevering and hardworking people poured in to do the work that Bermudians shunned. Now there are thousands of them, unobtrusively doing two days' work in one: planting, hoeing, growing vegetables, and creating beautiful gardens, and making an orderly, essential contribution to the life of the island. Governor Bruere brought in farm implements in the mid-eighteenth century, but Governor Reid, who took office in 1839, found only two elderly plows left on the island. Determined to push the people into working more satisfactorily on their land, he brought in about four dozen more plows and held plowing contests to persuade Bermudians that Farming is Fun. Thanks to him and the Portuguese, the island began to produce enough vegetables —finally.

Well into the nineteenth century, streets, though pleasantly shaded, were still unlit, dusty, unswept, and with no sidewalks. From the 1870's onwards there were many changes for the better, though sometimes at the sacrifice of trees. Lights first appeared on Front Street, then later on some other streets, and a red brick sidewalk was installed on Front Street in 1893. Before that pedestrians had taken their chances with horse buns and puddles —"Mud to the ankle and splashed to the waist" was how one visitor put it. Front Street consisted of dwellings upstairs, and little intriguing shops at street level, which attracted visitors as soon as they got off the boat. With the increased activity at the wharves it was thought considerate to erect covered sheds, and pride-of-India trees were planted, to make waiting and working more bearable for men and horses.

An occasional visit from a crowned head or a relative of one has given Bermuda a spur to civic facelifting, and she puts on an impressive turnout. Before Princess Louise's visit, houses, walls and roofs were freshly whitewashed (fewer colors were used then), verandahs were repaired to ensure the safety of parade-watchers and painted while the mood was on; flagstaffs were mended, or new ones put up; shopfronts were trimmed with flowers, and lampposts with more flags, lending the towns a musical-comedy atmosphere; roads and steps were swept and sprinkled; children drilled and sang; bandsmen perspired; horses were made glossy and carriages gleaming; little girls rehearsed how they would hand up a welcoming bouquet (after the Princess's visit the crimson broadcloth that covered the ferry steps was sold off in two-yard lengths); uniforms and harness were furbished; top hats, topees and toupées were spruced up; and elaborate arches of cedar and flowers were put across streets on the royal route.

But mostly nothing happened in Bermuda. While visitors placidly waited for something to turn up they watched sailboats in the harbor or Harrington Sound, or supervised loading and unloading at the wharves. When they were taken sailing by their expert hosts they kept a confident eye on the rocks that appear so close to the surface, that anyone not boasting a Bermuda helmsman wincingly waits to feel the scrape on the bottom. In rowboats they leaned over and gazed into the clear green water, speculated about the jewelled fish, and possibly thought of Tom Moore's sprinkle of the feathery oar that wing'd him round this fairy shore.

For more inward reflection there is nowhere like an old graveyard, and wandering round, surmising about the inhabitants, is a universal occupation of visitors. In some Bermuda churchyards there are marble gravestones, rather ornate, and looking a bit showy in contrast to the stark white boxes in which most deceased Bermudians lie, eight deep, in a simple limestone tomb. Sorrowing families sent these elaborate headstones from England to perpetuate the names of loved ones who had been lost at sea—it sounds so lonely—or in one of the yellow fever outbreaks.

Perhaps some other family member made the long voyage to that cluster of rocks in the middle of nowhere, and reaching it had been comforted to find the dead relative was resting in one of the earth's most beautiful places—a solace to the living, but a matter of total unconcern to the dead. No longer caring and no longer segregated are the slaves, some of whose bones lie equal, but separate, at St. Peter's, in St. George's, with simple markers, some bearing just a first name, at the western end of the churchyard. It has been claimed that this is so that when Gabriel blows his horn, the whites at the east end will be woken first and attain the kingdom of heaven ahead of their slaves.

Alive and tormented by their beautiful surroundings, yet unable to escape into them, were the thousands of men who worked creating Dockyard, at Ireland Island. In 1810, as a result of the decision to make a fortification and provisions center for the British Navy, Dockyard was begun by slaves and free blacks, directed by British engineers. The slaves came from Bermuda, the United States, and from French and Spanish possessions. Local men were hired from their owners, and of the others, some came as refugees from a political movement. All were provided with food, lodging, and clothing, and received quarterly wages. They worked as shipwrights, carpenters, smiths, masons, fitters, sailmakers, and in all the appropriate skilled or unskilled occupations.

By 1810 the number of convicts in England was alarming, and to avoid feeding and housing hundreds of them about a third were transported to the colonies, most going to Australia. By about 1820 the notion of slavery was beginning to be abhorrent, and this, combined with the greatly diminished population in Bermuda due to yellow fever, may have suggested the idea of using convict labor. Transportation was preferable to hanging, and in

1824 the first consignment was brought from England to erect magazines, fortifications, and other buildings, many of which can be seen today, with their handsome, time-defying style and excellent workmanship. In the next twenty years over 9000 men were brought in and were housed in shacks, and in hulks offshore. Yellow fever raged off and on, and more than 2000 of the convicts died and were buried on Ireland Island, and Watford and Long Islands, before their sentences were completed. Of the rest, all went back home in 1863 except William Facey, who was in Bermuda because he had purloined a horse of his father's and sold it. Not thinking the lad would be deported, the father turned him in. When his term was up, Facey was allowed to stay on and assume a legitimate interest in horses. He ran a mail-carrying coach between St. George's and Hamilton, and also the main livery stable, getting away with extravagant prices, according to one contemporary tourist. But perhaps the glamor attaching to the proprietor made it worth the outlay.

Just before the turn of the century, push bikes came into the island and visitors could bicycle—or tricycle—and stop whenever they felt like it, to absorb the beauty and the perfume of gardens, or watch a farmer with his hoe. If walking and bicycling seemed too strenuous, visitors in the Victorian era were driven in carriages named after the Queen or hired a drive-your-own-wayward-donkey cart. They went to admire the stalagmite organ pipes and buddhas in the caves; they took the horse bus somewhere along the line between St. George's and Somerset, or crossed the harbor in the ferry. They did gentle, nostalgic watercolors of cottages, sea, and oleanders; they lay in shady gardens filled with bird-embroidered sound; or they exposed a discreet amount of "limb" to be sun-ripened—for someone had decided that ultraviolet was good for the human

epidermis, and the sun cult was on. The first tennis court in the western hemisphere was built in Bermuda in 1873, and there was always croquet for the more circumspect, since ankles were not supposed to be shown in mixed company. Golf courses were created later, after World War I.

Visitors with acquaintances in the right quarters attended garrison balls. The island had nearly been annexed to America after the Revolutionary War, but the plans fell through. Instead, as she was situated between Halifax and the Bahamas, she was made into a British naval base, which from then on was reinforced every time Britain and the United States stalked wary circles round each other, and when the Kaiser's fleet was enlarged in the 1900's. Although wars seethed far away, Bermuda floated along, short of supplies, but not physically transmogrified until the 1940's when the U.S. Navy Base was created, devouring a tenth of the island and leaving St. David's Islanders dispossessed and weeping.

During war or peace, the local girls of every generation were entitled to their fertility ritual, and the garrison provided plenty of men to interest them. If supply ships were long overdue, the girls became resourceful, like Scarlett O'Hara, and made do with what they could find. Shabby shoes must be worn to yet another ball, or the wrong kind to a wedding, but everyone was in the same quandary. (Slaves frequently went barefoot, even to social events, to prolong the life of their shoes, which they slung round their shoulders until they arrived at the church or party). During hard times in the 1830's, when new ball gowns were out of the question, young ladies pulled the mosquito netting off their beds, had it heavily starched, and hoops inserted, and there was a reasonable facsimile of a new dressmaker-made dress. (A visitor at this time commented that the ladies frequently looked as if they were hewn out of rock salt). Next day a maid washed out the old-fashioned, non-permanent starch, and put the netting back over the bed.

In the average home the style of architecture is a pleasure to see. Built of limestone blocks, in the clean simple local style, they have tray ceilings, eyebrows over doors or windows, stepped chimneys and roofs, flared welcoming-arms steps, blinds to the windows and verandahs, and polished floors and massive beams of cedar. The older examples of these sturdy, wind-resisting houses were founded on the profits from the privateering and carrying trades, as were the captains' houses in New England, and as with them, the woodwork was executed by carpenters who had learned their trade in a boatyard and could really *build* a house.

However, inside they used to be rather comfortless in some respects. Rooms that boasted a fireplace could dispel the winter damp with a fire, yet in summer the kitchen was intolerable, even though the chimney was often outside. (Some large houses copied the Virginia system of having the kitchen in a separate building). Up to the twentieth century many houses had no outhouse, and as there were no screens, flies buzzed merrily and were part of the household. On summer nights a great deal of sleep time was thrown away in trying to smash the current generations of those maddening mosquitoes—a bloody splotch on the wall and a shout of triumph—and they were not brought under control until the U. S. Army attacked them in World War II.

The fragrant cedar was used for household furnishings from cradles and coffins to buckets and beds—at one time it was even wasted on pencils—and the local craftsmen made pieces of simple design that mingled peaceably with more ornate examples that were come by in one way or another, and which might also influence these craftsmen to make adaptations as they saw fit, if the brittle cedar would cooperate. Many houses have their treasures proudly displayed—beautiful furniture, glass, silver, and china, some of which was acquired in wrecking days by a strategy that is now only slightly embarrassing.

After slavery was eradicated, most of the housework was done by the family. The tropical habit of relaxed body movements made it a waste of effort to try and make people hurry. (This habit went well with the "drawl" that was deplored in the seventeenth century, and which was said to result from the difficulty of maintaining a pure English accent in the colonies on account of the influx of immigrants. Hearing the Bermudian version of English now provides one of the pleasures of returning). Still, the work got done; and in many houses a woman came in to help with laundry, cleaning, and the cooking which was done in iron pots that stood on convenient ledges in the fireplace, with cedar or sagebrush for fuel. The sea-rod was used for stirring, and as an egg beater in the preparation of cakes and puddings; the sea-fan, or huska, made a good sieve, or a scrubber for pots, pans and tables; dried porgy skin was used for scrubbing too, and made an adequate substitute for sandpaper. Until the present century Bermudians didn't use much milk, except for butter and buttermilk. Scallop shells made good skimmers for this, and they were used as well for emptying post holes. Laundry and dishes were often done at the beach to save fresh water.

From the earliest days of the colony, water was a constant difficulty. It was needed for everything, though not so much for drinking or washing, since early Bermudians did not share modern man's compulsion to boast an odor-free person. The first settlers would be accustomed to collecting rain in butts at home, and soon devised a system of cedar tanks and cisterns. As the island filled up with people it became a commendable local habit to see to it that taps did not dribble, or even drip, and that an awareness of the sacredness of water was instilled in each generation. But visitors, who are needed so badly by the economy, are not used to this conservation, and many of them squander water in horrible amounts, oblivious to the fact that it is a fundamental treasure to the island. In one way or another they have about 100 gallons per day, per person, poured out for them, which is a third of what the average Roman used when the Empire was at its peak and bathing was an elaborate art. But since it is not diplomatic to ask tourists to forego anything, Bermuda has continued researching the water table and has recently found added supplies in store. By 1932 Sir Harry Watlington had set up a system of wells that drew on the reservoir of fresh water that floats on the heavier sea water. Though brackish and unpotable, it was fine for flushing and washing. Now there is an extensive government plant and several hotels have systems of their own.

Guests have always enjoyed the restful gardens that look like pages from a flower catalog: too good to be true, but there they really are, making the beholder quicken with pleasure and with the desire to try and imitate at least some of the beauty in his own garden. The famous Bermuda lily was introduced in the 1850's by either a flower-loving sailor or a missionary returning from Japan. It thrived, but a new batch of bulbs brought in around the turn of the nineteenth century brought a deadly virus which took many years of dedicated research and labor to eradicate. Fortunately, the result was a lily plant that bloomed a month ahead of other kinds, from January to May. It became a major export, and is now the island's only agricultural one. Though the scent is cloying, the plant is so lovely one feels ashamed to carp about the perfume.

These soul-satisfying gardens have to be brought forth from the rock itself. It isn't possible just to plant a garden on Bermuda; it has to be wrestled into shape. First the space must be cleared by blasting and carving. In the process steps, seats, walls, and planters are created, all made of the indigenous limestone which hardens with continued exposure to the weather. Planting a tree or bush involves blasting a hole which causes cracks; then the tree spreads its roots wherever it can find a crevice for them, and takes hold. One reason the beautiful cedars survived so well against the persistent winds was their rare ability to finger their way down into the porous rock (sometimes in most unpromising places), to probe and hang on, twisted but secure. The *Juniperus bermudiana* had as many uses as the palmetto, and was far more enduring. Some trees grew to seventy feet at maturity, though it was not easy to find beams more than sixteen feet long, and this limited the width of houses. Up to a hundred species of birds sheltered in the cedars during their migrations. The dismaying blight of the early 1940's killed 80 per cent of the cedars in six years, and the birds and plants that depended on them suffered or died as a result.

The varying levels of the gardens used to give an enhancing impression of more space than there really was, thanks to views and surprise corners—all the result of seeming chance, but actually due to the artistry of their designers. Tom Moore gushed over the numerous little white houses glimpsed through vistas of trees. Now a tremendous number of extra corners have been built over with wings and cottages for the modern tourists, who flow in at a rate of 400,000 a year, and it is just as likely to be trees glimpsed through vistas of sugar-cube houses. But although there are not much more than eighteen square miles for the tourists themselves, there is still a comforting sense of individuality and breathing space. Houses may be close together, but there is a surprising illusion of privacy due to the constant rise and fall of terrain between one house and its neighbor.

There is an abundance of public and private gardens to choose from, but not quite all Bermuda gardens are designed to entrance the eye. Tucked away in the peaceful Botanical Gardens is the Garden for the Blind, designed and created about fifteen years ago by Lady Gladys Hall. To qualify for this garden, trees and plants need only smell fragrant or aromatic, or have leaves of interesting texture or shape. The paths of crushed local stone are simply laid out, and a square stone at each corner shows a change of direction. The plants are in raised borders and are identified in Braille on their labels. There is a childhood statue of Louis Braille, who was blind from the age of three. One of the wooden benches encircles a wide-flung camphor tree; a fountain tickles the ear as it splashes into a round pool, and birds complete the quiet idyll.

Or is it so quiet? Just as a stranger's first impression of New England spring might be the strident, demanding call of the handsome blue jay, so the new arrival in Bermuda cannot be there more than an hour without being aware of the kiskadee. The bird's presence is one of man's attempts to readjust the balance of nature. Two hundred specimens were brought from Trinidad in the spring and summer of 1957 in hopes that they would reduce the population of the anolis lizard which was eating the beetles which were brought in to eat the green scale that was infesting the oleanders… However, the kiskadee isn't all that keen on lizards, unless there's not much else to choose from.

Playing favorites, one can't be sorry that he found Bermuda's cicadas, grasshoppers, dragonflies, or even minnows (who were doing *their* best to control mosquito larvae) more to his taste. There was at first some doubt that *Tyrannus sulphuratus* would be happy in the relatively severe winters of Bermuda, but he has obviously taken a firm hold on the island, has increased—he raises an irresistible orange crest in courtship—and lives peaceably with bluebirds, cardinals, and the rest. From his favorite perch in large shade trees the kiskadee screams his name in a loud, penetrating voice, and his plumage puts him among the most conspicuous two-legged creatures on the island.

Considerable caution is needed when introducing a brand-new element into a small space. With carriages, ferries, and bicycles the island seemed well equipped with transportation. Then in 1931 a delightful little railway was built—after much heated debate in Parliament—and the picture seemed complete. But the railway turned out to be a story in itself. The track was never properly laid, and there were places where the train would buck. Not only did some of the passengers catch their breath at the stunning views, but they would hold it when going over the trestles, not realizing that these were stronger than many other sections of the line. There was a place below the lighthouse where the engine driver could see the coral pouring down the cliff, and he would wonder when the whole thing was going to break away—which it finally did with fatal results. The system cost more than any other railway, always ran at a loss, and was finally sold to British Guiana (now Guyana).

It is human nature to suffer from fidgets once in a while, after seeing what somebody else enjoys, and naturally some Bermudians wanted a car. In 1908 a Scarlet Runner was brought in, but firmly shipped out again the same year. Even governors were denied a car, and in the late 1930's the gentleman holding that position was so put out at being refused one that he resigned. Doctors were permitted cars, as was right and proper, but visitors saw Bermuda as a gem that should be left in a simple setting. Early in the twentieth century Woodrow Wilson sent a petition to the Bermuda Legislature, bearing 112 signatures, including that of Samuel L. Clemens. It said: "We, the undersigned, visitors to Bermuda, venture respectfully to express the opinion that the admission of automobiles to the Island would alter the whole character of the place in a way which would seem to us very serious indeed… The danger to be apprehended is chiefly from reckless tourists who would care nothing for local opinion or for the convenience and safety of others. This is one of the last refuges now left in the world to which one can come to escape such persons. It would, in our opinion be a fatal error to attract to Bermuda the extravagant and sporting set who have made so many other places entirely intolerable to persons of taste and cultivation."

A farmer in the English Lake District put it this way, concerning his own part of the world: "Whaur's the hurry? There's worse ways o' travel than sittin' behint a steady horse an' snuffin' fresh air instead o' stinkin' petrol… These days they rush here and rush there an' pass on sae quick, they see nowt." But Bermuda found cars irresistible. Although she has been accused of being infatuated with the past, she had an alert eye on the future when she allowed cars to enter in 1946, after more heated debate. But they only squeezed in by a majority of one vote, so there were many eyes who saw with commendable clarity what the future might bring, and the Legislature sagely denied permits to visitors—even those who are neither extravagant nor sporting. A hundred years ago Mark

Twain was already apprehensive of "the triple curse of railways, telegraphs, and newspapers" but he returned many times to Bermuda since it was a pleasing step back into the past. If he could see his island now he would be disappointed in his local friends' decision, and resolve to find a refuge somewhere else, if he could.

To return and find the place transformed and taken over by traffic is to suffer two days' culture shock. Many of the old images, carried in memory, turn out to have been totally inaccurate for years, like a stored picture discovered to be cracked and distorted. There's a refusal to discard the illusion. The mind says "No! It can't be. If I look again it won't have happened." This reaction to island traffic is puzzling to the local young, who never knew their little country when it was called "the Isles of Rest." Now the young fellows stand about discussing their vehicles, just as in any other community. Edmund Waller wrote: "None sickly lives, or dies before his time" and Richard Stafford: "As to the age when they dye, 'tis age and weakness that is the cause, and not any disease that attends them." Short of exercise, and possibly with less lovely legs than in the cycle era, Bermudians' time comes sooner now, and they are able to die of the same distresses and strains as the rest of civilized humanity.

There's a stream of traffic and a sense of hurry in town and on busy roads, with riders buzzing by wearing helmets and abstracted looks. Scarcely a month passes without a fatal accident. The air is full of snarling sounds and exhaust fumes; as well as attractive floral road signs, there are parking problems and radar detectors; well over 300 unarmed police are needed to cope with traffic and the ubiquity of the population. The island has shrunk, but curiously, some people who have a machine to take them to work can't seem to get there on time. When they walked or cycled, they were punctual. Along the main roads it is no longer recommended to stop just anywhere to admire a garden, as there's apprehension that a vehicle will bear down on you. The dizzying rate of 20 m.p.h. (that's what the sign says), feels more threatening in miniature surroundings. Yet in the evening, after most traffic has gone home, the air is clean, the fumes have blown out to the long-suffering sea, the flowers can be smelled again, and the crickets have no competitors for their din.

But looking regretfully over the shoulder is useless. A mild form of sophistication has been imposed on Bermuda, and it's too late for the simple life. New phenomena become absorbed; innovations prove acceptable, are admitted to be advantageous, and soon prove indispensable.

Bermuda is a paradise threatened, but not yet spoiled. Many of the old sounds and smells are still there: the breeze moving through the tall grasses; the restless rattling of the palm trees; flowers still assail the nose in intoxicating waves of perfume; there is still the occasional clip-clop of hooves and even a whiff of horse manure for old time's sake, as there are some Victorias for tourists who want a leisurely sight-see, unimpeded by car windows, and there has been a tremendous increase in the horse population for riding and racing. Bermuda still gently persuades visitors to relax and enjoy their stay. Tranquility can still be found, but the search is a bit longer. Get off busy roads, find a lane, lean your (motorized) wheel, and sit in the sun. Shed any thoughts of "civilization" and "progress" and abandon yourself to the warmth until you become dozy. As you meditate, the nostalgic tinkling bicycle bell can no longer be heard in the land, but the sounds to reach you will be a gentle lapping of water, the swish of branches, and the skittering of a dry leaf as the breeze pushes it across the path. This much-loved island still has abundant beauty, but it must never be taken for granted. Paradise, please take care.

Church, Shelly Bay

Street cleaner, St. George's

Bus driver

Palmetto in Fort Hamilton moat

Water catchment

Spanish Point

St. George's

Smith, near Spittal Pond
1976

Farmer's daughter,
circa 1942

Near Surf Bay

Pitt's Bay Roa

Somerset rooftop

St. David's Lighthouse keep

◄ *Ruin and cedar*

◄ *Tucker's Town Bay*

Far